Linnea—

you've been such a
blessing in my life
I'm happy we walked
part of this journey together,
your spirit will be missed
and your loving energy
never forgotten. These driftwood
earrings remind me of
angel wings — I can't
think of a more fitting
pair — as you are an
angel in my life.
I love you
Jamie

—

I stand on the mountains that, this morning, were my horizon. Here, the world feels both attainable and unreachable. Conquerable and impossible. Vast, but also tiny.

—

the desert

APRIL 28

It feels like every ache and pain any hiker has ever felt is manifesting in my body right now.

APRIL 30

Syd and I woke up in the freezing cold rain. We wondered what we got ourselves into.

MAY 3

I was so hungry, I cried when I started eating. A whole jar of peanut butter later, we hiked five more miles to camp.

MAY 5

I wanted to write today. I wanted to write about what it felt like to be walking through the desert. I wanted to write about the moment I realized life is still happening for other people while I am walking and forced to make it to the next water source, the next camp site. Every step hurts, and I walk on. The pain felt in my feet becomes a hesitation before every step. Our second 15 mile day was easier than the first. We got to the water source and it was a trickle out of a faucet. We spent an hour and a half filling 6 liters of water each knowing we have 20 miles until the next water source. We found extra water on the way from trail angels and a bag of three Granny Smith apples to split between five hikers. We sat under an overpass in the shade and enjoyed each juicy bite. Sounds of laughter fill our breaks and we snack and chat with each other. We are all thankful for this rest, knowing we have to hike another six miles. But we don't think about hiking, we're completely in the moment of sweet apple juice and shade. Nothing else matters. It feels like it's the way we're supposed to live – full attention in each moment. We pack up our home every morning and set it up in a new spot that night. Tonight, we are in a canyon in the middle of a mountain. It feels like a movie set in a desert in Arizona. We took off our shoes and stuck our feet in the sand while we set up camp. There's beautiful desert rock on each side of us lined with cactus and yucca plants. The colors are muted beautiful light browns and reds.

MAY 11
I used my knife for the first time – to cut cheese.

MAY 16
Yesterday, we walked toward civilization and I could feel nature disappear. The trash increased. I was shocked seeing an empty 2L of soda, then I come to realize that is just the beginning of seeing society's attitude toward earth. One of selfishness and carelessness.

MAY 29

We've come to realize – if you want something, just ask. People are always willing and wanting to help.

> *"Independence robs somebody of their ability to feel magnificent"*

MAY 31

There are flies buzzing in my ears, face, and mouth. We lay on a picnic table and eat hot dogs that are accompanied with flattened buns and ketchup packets. The air is perfect. It smells fresh, woodsy, and hot. Yesterday I called Jason, my brother, for his birthday. We only talked for a few minutes. It's interesting to think that life still goes on when mine feels to be on hold. My body hurts and my pack is heavy and I don't want to leave this picnic table under the trees. The smell of burning sage settles my thoughts and stops time. There is no place I'd rather be. We hike past day hikers and I feel bad that they have to go back home after a few miles. I'm so lucky to be able to hike past them and stay out here for months.

JUNE 1

I like packing my bag everyday. It is a fun challenge to make it well balanced, because if it's not, you'll suffer the rest of the day. There's a certain type of quality, time and focus it requires.

> *"How you do anything is how you do everything."*

JUNE 5

Hiker Heaven provides guitars and good vibes. We sat 21 people on hay bails around a fire pit. We all sang camp songs. Bed time came at midnight and we cowboy

camped for our first time (no tent, just a sleeping bag
outside). It's such an incredible feeling to truly sleep
under the stars. They stretched across the black moonless
sky. Each constellation telling its story just by shining.
It feels like summer.

JUNE 13
Night hiking is a must in the desert. Since sight is
limited to a five yard circle with a head lamp, it seems as
if the other senses are stronger. My ears became domi-
nant. My eyes were seeing only what my headlamp chose
to show me. The shadows are bigger than the bugs so
don't be scared. I do miss the scenery though, but it's
nice to escape the heat for a few miles.

JUNE 18
This morning I woke up to hundreds of ants on my shirt
and shorts and in my boots. De-anting took a while.
Next time – hang clothes in tree.

JUNE 19
The first green grass we've seen on trail. I lay in a meadow surrounded by tall pine trees. There's a certain smell
here; earthy yet fresh. I am eating poofy Cheetos, a gift
from a couple of trail angels. Days pass slower out here.
There is an abundance of time and life. I stare into the
night sky as the stars appear and remember this feeling.
A tangible type of quietness lowers over the forest and
my mind meets it.

JUNE 20
We walk into the sunrise with the full moon following
behind us. The bees are buzzing around newly blooming
bushes and I walk over a line of ants. Lizards spin out in

the dirt as they scurry away from my trekking poles. I think about how many people have walked this path. Souls from all over the world have traveled this step by step. I wonder if they have experienced the pain I have, and I wonder if they've felt the joy I have. The trail unites people, it brings everyone to the same experience. We easily sympathize and connect with other hikers, knowing they've walked every step we have. Everyone is equal out here. Equally smelly, equally dirty, equally hot, and equally thirsty. A type of unity that is only found in the wild.

the sierras

JUNE 29

I'm listening to my new favorite Fruition song, *"Come On, Get In."* I put it on repeat. It's the type of song that makes me memorize this moment. I memorize this quiet feeling inside me. I think of those who have never known this feeling. I should be writing about what happened a few days ago, but I don't want to leave this moment. I don't want to willingly leave my personal bliss. I'm at peace. I finally understand why the mountains/forests/trees are such a sanctuary for people – after living in the desert, after walking 17 miles for shade, my thirst for shade seemed unquenchable. I've always thought trees knew the meaning of life. I think anything that's able to feel life's duality knows the meaning of life. Trees experience all weather – snow, wind, rain, sun. The ocean - calm, swells, currents, rain, sun. Even me, that's what we're doing out here – exposing ourselves to earth's elements. One no less than the other. Fully experiencing life's duality and contrast and pushing through each extreme without judgment or expectation.

JULY 3

We are camped in the most beautiful meadow. Tall trees and deer and cute little marmots. I just looked at my feet and my pinky toe nail is hollow and will soon come off. My legs are so ashy and covered with mosquito bites. My butt too... I remember my Popa saying, *"scratch it if it itches, even if it's in your britches."*

JULY 5

We summited Mt. Whitney. 14,505 feet in elevation, it is the tallest peak in the lower 48 states. I've never felt more powerful.

JULY 7

Today I fell in a river and smashed my face into a
rock which resulted in a wet boot and a bloody nose.
I couldn't stop laughing.

JULY 8

I sit on a huge granite rock in the shape of a perfect
recliner. The breeze is cool on my hot skin. A waterfall is
the only thing I hear. I walked by a few marmots today. I
stop and stare at them and they look at me like they have
something to say.

JULY 9

Rae Lakes. Glen Pass. Syd caught a fish. I lay in the grass.
The one cloud in the sky just moved in front of the sun, a
huge shadow that moves across the lake. The wind picks
up and creates white caps on the water. Then, just as
quickly as they came, they disappear. Stillness and warmth
return. I sit and enjoy the contrast of the gray jagged
mountains and the flat, blue lake below. The green trees
that line the lake stand tall in all their glory. Today
we've seen some of the most beautiful lakes. Colors I
dream of present themselves in liquid form. The clearest
and cleanest water we've seen on the trail yet. The
water looks like Hawaii but there is no salt in the air. I
miss the smell of the ocean.

JULY 14

When we finally make it to town for a shower, we use
shampoo as body wash and splurge on conditioner. One
blade razors are useless and lotion is mandatory. It takes
a few minutes of pain to run a brush though our hair.
It feels softer than it's ever been. Who knew that being
clean was such a luxury.

JULY 19

When we summited Glen Pass ten days ago, we received
applause and cheer from ladies at the top. There are so
many women out here. It's been really amazing to see

– but to also represent it is an incredible feeling. People have so many questions and we receive support from everyone we chat with. Support comes in all forms – an encouraging word, a high five, a bag of peanut m&m's, a ride, a wave, a smile, a pitcher of beer, or a box in the mail. All of these gestures are how we've made it this far. We're giving ourselves to this journey, opening ourselves to a world of possibility. We're ready to handle, deal with, and experience anything the universe has ready for us.

JULY 20

We hiked Muir Pass a few days ago. It was easy to lose the trail because of the amount of snow that was still there. The biggest feeling of relief was experienced the moment I saw a footprint in the snow – *"Thank God someone has been here."* The path is marked by rare rock stacks. This pass was the first time that I felt truly alone and out in the middle of nowhere. I'd look around and see glaciers and mountains and lakes and streams. And no one else. Just me in this vast land that to some would be scary, but for me it was comforting. I breathed in deeply, all the air my body could hold. Silence.

JULY 21
A teenage girl told us we are her heroes.

JULY 22

I just pulled a bloody dead mosquito from my scalp. This is not the first time...

JULY 24

The sun has set but the night sky has yet to appear. Soft light lands on our tent and keeps me from falling asleep. I think of the weight we carry on our backs everyday. It's a miracle we're still standing.

JULY 26

This morning, my PopTart was so squished I had to eat it with my spork.

JULY 29

My parents came down to Yosemite and spent a few days with us. Having them here made me realize how much has happened. It's been a long walk. We said goodbye with pictures, hugs, tears, and I love yous. We had such a great time together. Every time I hug my mom, I feel a life's worth of her love. All the love she's ever loved, merges into this one moment. It's healing. It's comforting. It's powerful. Everything is okay. I walk away with strength to continue on this challenging adventure.

northern california

JULY 30

Syd naps next to me. Flies land on me and I let them
stay. I look in the distance and see bushes rustling in
the wind. The wild flowers have been beautiful purples,
oranges, yellows, and pinks. I smell wild mint. The sun
hits my face and my eyes squint to see. The more time
I spend out here, the less time exists. I watch the trees
for hours, everything is perfect here. It was this perfect
before I came, and will be just as perfect once I leave.
The wind never stops tickling the tree branches, the
water never stops flowing, the flies never stop flying. It
feels like I'm experiencing eternity. Time is unlimited
in nature. I finally feel part of it.

JULY 31

I'm laying on my stomach eating a caramel apple pop.
I see ants walking in the dirt and crawling on my mat.
What is their purpose? Dragon flies fly over Lilypad
Lake. We sit at mile 1,063 and enjoy our lunch in the
shade with a view of the water. A few minutes ago, a
yellow fly kept biting me. When I ran away, it chased
me and bit me again. Why is he out to get me? Earlier
today, our friend BrewHiker (he brews beer on trail
with different wild herbs he finds) got exciting news
about an opportunity to be featured on the Brew Net-
work. It was his dream, coming true. This sparked
excitement within me. Excitement for the future and
for endless possibilities that are waiting to happen. I

love when life feels new and fresh. Open and expansive. I will keep this feeling and these thoughts with me. It is fun to think that life is limitless. Once we rid ourselves of all that we think defines us, that's when we can feel the freedom we crave. Let go.

AUGUST 4

We walked into a neon green forest. Moss thriving on only half of every tree. A few miles later, we descend into Echo Lake, the most beautiful mountain lake ever. Truly paradise. They offered a boat taxi to the other side of the lake, but I can promise you the hike was better. We walked on granite and sand, around the lake the whole way. Tall beautiful pine trees stood above us and we saw dream house status cabins. It was hot and the weather was perfect. It was the kind of peace that lasted all day.

AUGUST 15

My mom came down to visit again. She hiked with me a little, then we split ways. She hiked south to her camp-site and I hiked north to find mine. We are 7.7 aerial miles away, 14.5 trail miles. She is probably doing to same thing as me right now. Laying in her tent and wishing we were still together. Saying goodbye to her is difficult every time. I'll just accept that it'll never be easy. She's done so much for me, yet again. I struggle with ways to thank her and I feel like I can never say I love you enough. Her hugs remind me that I can conquer the world. They contain so much love and belief – it's overwhelming so I just cry. I can't wait to love my children this much and I can only hope to impact their life like she has mine.

AUGUST 16

I was out of camp by 6:40am. The first person on the trail.
How did I know this? I quickly became dressed with
spider webs. Invisible to the eye, I'd feel each web attach
itself across my face, mouth, forehead, and sometimes in
my eye lashes. I'm decorated with natures intricate
designs. Northern California becomes more beautiful
with every step. The trees are tall and the pine cones big.
Mt. Shasta presents herself capped with snow. This
mountain is stunning. It stands on top of hills full of
trees. The contrast is magnificent. It's stamped into the
blue sky, forever on the horizon. I'm at camp and there is
no one else here. It's just me and the buzzing bugs and
singing birds. I find myself scared. Since we skipped 250
miles of the trail, these forests are new to me. I did not
walk into this section like I had all the others. I hear an
animal run through the forest. I hope it's just a deer...
This place is new and I am feeling a little uneasy. I try to
calm myself and enjoy the night. I pull out the Prophet
to read a few poems.

> *"and forget not that the earth delights to feel your bare feet*
> *and the winds long to play with your hair."*
> Khalil Gibran

AUGUST 17

The flies are back. The snakes are back. The heat is back. The thirst is back. I want to cry. I want to scream. Get me out of here. GET ME OUT OF HERE!!! I'm done. It's over. I just want to press exit, or end game. As if this were something I could instantly escape. Take me away, out of California. I am done with the desert. I'm done.

AUGUST 18

I wake up to silence, as if the whole forest is still asleep. I realized, even nature can only interact with me in my frustration, annoyance, and uneasiness. If I'm scared, it will show me every reason why I should be scared. It will match my annoyance and my irritation. It will provide experiences that mirror the way I'm feeling. It will give me reasons to justify my shitty attitude and will help me prove my limitations – only if this is what I want. There's only one way to step out of this cycle. Become settled and relaxed. Distract myself. Think about something else. Listen to the birds sing. Laugh at my situation. Have fun with it. This too, shall pass.

AUGUST 19

I sit pressed against a stack of rocks. With the sun behind me, it is the only shade. There's a slight breeze and only the things near me are moving – the tiny weeds and clusters of dead grass. Everything else is still, like a picture. The clouds don't even move. They are permanently floating over Mt. Shasta. Dragonflies own the sky. I look at the trail and see it zig zag down to the valley where we came from. It's been a climb I've been dreading all day, +6,600 ft. But, I didn't know it was gonna be this. I didn't know it was gonna be this beautiful. One of the most amazing and memorable views yet. It's so glorious and huge. And mesmerizing. I watch a tiny white spec slowly move along the ridge trail. He will be here soon enough and the view of Castle Crags will be worth it all. Worth the pain, the heat, and the struggle. It looks like a castle, it does. Medieval and wondrous. And to think, before yesterday, I didn't even know it existed. It's spooky to realize just how small my world is. But it leaves access for surprise and utter fascination. I like my small world because it's easy to blow my mind. It's quiet up here on this ridge. No one knows I'm here and I kinda like it.

oregon

SEPTEMBER 3

I eat skittles. There's blood on my leg and my feet hurt. I've eaten almost all my food. Hunger I never thought possible came knocking on the door. We woke up to frost this morning. It was so damn cold, almost laughable. I don't even want to know how cold it will be in a month. We walked a marathon yesterday. Oregon, so far, proves to be pretty flat. We've walked through so much forest that I'm still shocked when I see something new. Huckleberries fill my hand as we stop and take a break for another harvest.

SEPTEMBER 5

I lay in my sleeping bag, bundled in all my clothes. Preparing for another night that will hopefully come with more sleep and less shivers. Yesterday was Crater Lake. I look at pictures and the view is stunning, it looks like a fake back drop. The blue of the lake is royal and bright. Wind patterns appeared on the water in lines, like sand on the bottom of the ocean.

SEPTEMBER 7

There are three types of trees in Oregon: standing, fallen, or burnt.

SEPTEMBER 8

A sense of tranquility keeps growing. Like roots in the ground, it is not visible. Only felt. I collect moments of

stillness and peace and recall them often, as if they have
more wisdom to share with me. The quiet, empty moments have the most to give. I reach with an open hand
towards that I do not understand. Someday, I want to
hold the knowledge that was once inaccessible. Have it
sit in my palm and see it as it is, a glimmer of light. It
too, can only be felt to be understood.

SEPTEMBER 13

I have a hard time sleeping when things aren't right. The
silence is loud and the energy heavy and low. I don't
know why I'm able to sense it so well. But every time it's
off, it's sickening. I feel stuck and unable to move regardless of how far I walk each day. The progress I once
made seems to disappear with each mile. Maybe I need
to follow suit; allow my ego to disappear with every
step. As I walk out of who I was, I walk into all I want
to become. I walk into feelings of clarity and peace. I
walk into promises of expression and freedom. Into love
and acceptance of life, for it gave birth to all that I am.
My new desires will demand focus and accountability.
I need to follow my truth despite all who disagree.

SEPTEMBER 14

We walked through Mt. Jefferson Wilderness Area today.
The beauty astounds me. A mountain with snow caps
that had different dimensions in each direction. The gray
rock, pure white snow, and bright sky came together
into, what is now, a beautiful memory. The mountain was
enormous, the biggest thing we've seen in Oregon so
far. I write to recall the beauty and peace the mountain
held. It's purpose so clear. To stand and be. I wonder if
it holds any secrets dear to it. I wonder what that moun-

tain means to people, what kind of trust it holds. It seemed to be the keeper of something special. This may be all I ever know.

SEPTEMBER 15

I'm learning to adopt the pace of nature. Patterns of patience exist in the forest. The sunrise never comes too early, nor the sunset too late. Each day begins with a miracle and the few who witness it are the lucky ones. To live outside is to be free. As a society, we've been accustomed to sheltering ourselves from the very thing we need. Without experiencing the seasons like humans used to, we miss a deep connection to ourselves. We've been creating a lifestyle to make us more comfortable. It's interesting though, we are more uncomfortable than ever. There's an ongoing search for happiness which seems to always be just out of reach. However, if we can return to nature, all would be solved. It's a medley of connection between the body, mind, and spirit. When the body is exposed to the elements, it demands a sense of comfort that is impossible to find indoors. Experience is knowledge. And knowledge is comfort.

SEPTEMBER 17

Accompanied by the changing leaves, autumn brings frozen mornings and a cool afternoon breeze. I watch how the plants show time, they live according to the seasons. The Japanese maples seem to be one of the first to show their colors, healthy greens change to fluorescent oranges and reds that glow. It's the start of something beautiful. We walk with autumn on our heels and chase the end of summer. It's a thrill to watch it disappear day

by day. Fall is a season I've forgotten. To view it with
new eyes, something only few get to experience. How
lucky am I.

SEPTEMBER 20
The sound of the endless Ramona Falls makes me ques-
tion the notion of time. Unsure of its properties. But
certain that it's only measured linearly. Life is not two
dimensional – how is it that it's recorded that way? Time
lines, pictures, even our memories seem to be categorized
chronologically. Memories should be based more on
emotion and less on time.

washington

SEPTEMBER 24

We got to camp early today. It felt like we got off work
early and had a whole day to rest in our tent. Dry from
the rain and cozy in our sleeping bags, we cooked food
and realized our hike is almost over. We think about
all the stuff we deal with. It feels nice knowing we'll,
soon, never have to deal with it again. Though, all these
things represent a certain time in our life. A time when
we walked all day long and laughed about nothing. A
time when our days were broken up into water sources.
Where 20 miles was easy. A time when food rations and
hiker hunger was a scary combination. As much as I
want this hike to be over, I don't. There are so many
undesirable things we deal with, but for some reason I
don't want them to end. They provide acceptance and
humility. It's taught me that all things are temporary and
without the bad, there is no good. The duality is what's
so fulfilling.

SEPTEMBER 25

There are birds, and man do they sing. They are just
happy here. There weren't these song birds in California
or Oregon. I noticed them our first day in Washington.
We sit at a picnic table. It's something we've missed while
being out here – a seat. We are so grateful to actually sit
upright. And when we do, it's the best feeling in the
world. I watch the shadows pass as the sun moves around
the trees. I like the way life feels when I'm sitting at a

picnic table. The miles pass fast now. We no longer feel overwhelmed when we look at how far we have to go. We now feel like our luck is running out, like we want it to be longer. We're not quite ready to be done yet. Just give us another state to walk through.

SEPTEMBER 29

The first view of Mt. Rainier was shocking. I didn't even know we were so close, or maybe the mountain is just that huge. It is truly one of the most beautiful sights. I'm home. The fall leaves and warm afternoon feel so friendly. Winds rustle the trees in ways that sound specific to Washington. We sit with a view of four mountains. To the north – Mt. Rainier. To the west – we stand at the base of Mt. Adams. South – Mt. Hood. East – Mt. St. Helens. The sight was incredible, but the feeling even better. I felt accomplished and settled.

OCTOBER 2

There's so much more to these feelings than just starting a new chapter in my life. There's more to these feelings than ending a chapter in the same book. It feels premature and sudden. I think it would feel this way regardless. Whether we made it to Canada or not. The feelings would be the same. Maybe this is the post trail depression as described to me earlier. I'm not sure how to handle society just yet. The mountains raise my spirit and show me my strength. I want to feel this way in any place I live. This type of contentment and confidence is one thing I've walked long enough to receive. To stand tall and strong in who I am, just like the trees do everyday. Unwavering and rooted to their ground. I've watched them long enough to adopt their perspective. They witness life everyday with silence and acceptance. It's profound the lessons they speak.

OCTOBER 4

We set up the tent for the last time. Pulled out our sleeping
bags and made our pillows for the last time. The rain is
falling and the puddles are growing. What do I do when
I don't want to be finished hiking. I want to make it to
Canada. I'm so close. It might be a couple miserable weeks,
but I'd do it. I could handle it and I feel prepared for it.
But the weather and trail conditions are so unexpected,
it's hard to know what I'm walking in to. Is it worth
putting my life at risk? Obviously not. Weather is always
worst in the mountains, and this part of the trail is
inaccessible by car. There's no trail junctions to dirt roads,
it's all back country. The only way out is to walk 100
miles to the next highway. So as much as I don't want to
stop hiking, there's no guarantee of making it out of
there alive. It is between life and death and at this point,
we have to make the safe decision. We are home, Chinook
Pass is home. And we've walked home.

We did it!

We're here!

home

OCTOBER 27

I sit here, on the couch at home, pressing buttons and typing words on a screen. I don't even understand how this works. Technology is so advanced that I cannot fathom how it will keep evolving. But still, humans find ways to improve and create beyond my imagination. Where does their creation come from? Is there a special place they go to grab the newest idea? Are ideas born out of inspiration? Or do ideas come out of laziness or the feeling of lack? Technically, whichever way they come about, they're both still ideas that keep society at a constant progression. But, if these ideas come to us different ways, does each type of idea hold the same value? These questions rise up within me as I'm introduced back into civilization. I look at people's every day lives and see things I've lived without for five months. Useless things have become necessities. I am unwilling to adopt this lifestyle. I don't want to mold myself into accepting these commonalities. This unwillingness also brings a feeling of disconnection. There seems to be a separation between my mind and values and what society thinks is important. I feel unsure on what to do, knowing that I need to, in some ways, conform and play the game for a little bit. So, I sit here for just a bit longer and realize my trip is really over. I find myself wandering. Wandering through the house, wandering through my mind, wandering with no place to go. Without having to walk 25 miles today, I have so much time. I don't know what to get started on. I feel lost and purpose-less. I find confusion indoors. The day is so open and I struggle finding a path to follow. Instead of one trail that leads north, there are millions of roads that lead millions of places. I will go outside to find clarity, hoping to come back with some ideas of the direction I want my life to go.

On trail, the only book that was worth the weight was *"The Prophet"* by Khalil Gibran. When I read his poems, the words rose off the page. They'd crawl up my sleeve and I would feel them all over my skin. His language was powerful and brought life down to the simplest terms, reminding me that there are only a few things that really matter. In my current state of confusion, I reach for this book again. I am reminded that silence is the only teacher. It's funny that I offer so many words.

"For thought is a bird of space, that in a cage of words may indeed unfold its wings but cannot fly."
Khalil Gibran.

Made in the USA
San Bernardino, CA
21 February 2018